T0012228

FIRST IN FLIGHT

HOW A PHOTOGRAPH CAPTURED THE TAKEOFF OF THE WRIGHT BROTHERS' FLYER

By Michael Burgan

Consultant: Larry E. Tise, Department of History,
East Carolina University

COMPASS POINT BOOKS
a capstone imprint

Captured History is published by Compass Point Books, an imprint of Capstone.
1710 Roe Crest Drive
North Mankato, Minnesota 56003
www.capstonepub.com

Copyright © 2021 by Capstone. All rights reserved. No part of this publication may be reproduced in whole or in part, or stored in a retrieval system, or transmitted in any form or by any means, electronic, mechanical, photocopying, recording, or otherwise, without written permission of the publisher.

Library of Congress Cataloging-in-Publication Data is available on the Library of Congress website.
ISBN: 978-0-7565-6613-5 (library binding)
ISBN: 978-0-7565-6657-9 (paperback)
ISBN: 978-0-7565-6621-0 (ebook PDF)

Summary: On-point historical photographs combined with strong narration bring the story of the historic first flight ever to life. Kids will feel as though they are at Kill Devil Hills with Wilbur and Orville Wright as the brothers prepare to test their aircraft. They'll also learn about the history of flight and the skepticism that greeted the Wrights when they, at first, refused to release the photograph of their successful flight.

Image Credits
Getty Images: Bettmann, 26, 35, Corbis/Library of Congress, 37, Popperfoto, 52, SSPL, 16, ullstein bild Dtl., 15; Library of Congress: cover, 5, 6, 7, 10, 12, 13, 18, 20, 25, 27, 29, 31, 33, 34, 39, 42, 43, 46, 48, 54, 56 (top), 57, 58, 59 (bottom left), Manuscript Division/Wilbur Wright and Orville Wright papers, 1809-1979, 9, 21, 36, 56 (bottom), Prints and Photographs Division/Photographs in Carol M. Highsmith's America Project in the Carol M. Highsmith Archive, 55, 59 (bottom right); National Archives and Records Administration: 49, 59 (top); Shutterstock: Everett Historical, 23

Editorial Credits
Editor: Michelle Bisson; Designer: Tracy McCabe; Media Researcher: Svetlana Zhurkin; Production Specialist: Kathy McColley

Consultant Credits
Consultant: Larry E. Tise, Department of History, East Carolina University

All internet sites appearing in back matter were available and accurate when this book was sent to press.

Printer and bound in the USA.
PA117

TABLEOFCONTENTS

ChapterOne
READY TO TAKE FLIGHT

The wind at Kill Devil Hills on North Carolina's Outer Banks blew at about 20 miles (32 kilometers) per hour, and the temperature was just above freezing. It was December 17, 1903—much later than usual in the year for brothers Wilbur and Orville Wright to be at this stretch of beach. These sand dunes and the surrounding shore were near the tiny town of Kitty Hawk. Since 1900, the brothers had come to the area to test gliders they had designed at their bicycle shop in Dayton, Ohio. Though the bicycle business provided good income, what the brothers really wanted to do was sail through the air, not roll along roads on their bikes. They pursued flight together, as they had done so much else. As Wilbur once said, "From the time we were little children my brother Orville and myself lived together, played together, worked together and, in fact, thought together."

The idea of humans trying to fly was not new to the Wright brothers. Fascinated by the idea of flight, Wilbur, who was now 36, and Orville, four years younger, had spent many long hours studying how it could be done. They built models and then full-size gliders. Sometimes they argued over whose ideas were right, but they always remained a team. And their flights at Kill Devil Hills helped them improve their designs.

Wilbur and Orville Wright took turns flying in the gliders they built. This shows Wilbur making a right turn in a glider at Kill Devil Hills.

THE GLIDING GERMAN

Otto Lilienthal was a pioneer of human flight, building gliders that looked something like butterflies.

Otto Lilienthal assembled his first glider when he was still a teenager. That glider didn't fly, but the setback didn't stop him from pursuing human flight. Lilienthal, a German mechanical engineer, was one of the aviators who inspired the Wrights. Starting in 1890, he built more than a dozen gliders and made about 2,000 flights. He was sometimes called "the Flying Man." Across Europe and the United States, others bought and flew the German's gliders or built their own based on his design. By 1896, Lilienthal was a world leader in the field of aeronautics. Sadly, Lilienthal broke his back in a glider crash that same year. He died the next day.

Wilbur Wright saw a newspaper article about the great aviator's death. He later said that reading about Lilienthal's attempts to fly renewed an interest in flying he had first felt as a child. Wright said, "Lilienthal not only thought, but acted; and in doing so probably made the greatest contribution to the solution of the flying problem that has ever been made by any one man."

By the end of 1902, the brothers were ready to take the next step in aviation. They had proven that they could fly with their glider. But longer flights would require an aircraft that carried its own power source. Cars powered by gas engines were becoming popular, and the Wrights decided that one of those internal combustion engines could turn their glider into a powered aircraft.

When the Wrights couldn't find an engine both light and powerful enough for their needs, they turned to Charlie Taylor. He was a master mechanic in their bike shop, and he could make the precise

The 1903 engine built by Charlie Taylor

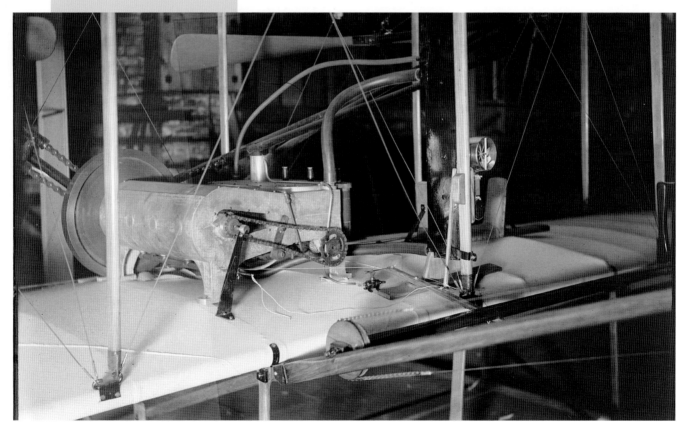

parts the brothers needed for both their cycles and their flying machines. The three men worked together on the engine, discussing the design and making sketches of the parts. Then Taylor went to work crafting the parts while the brothers worked on the frame of the aircraft.

It took Taylor six weeks to build the engine. Using aluminum for a major part of the engine made it light. Taylor was able to give the Wrights an engine even lighter than what they had hoped for. That would make it easier to stay in the air. It also produced more power, cranking out 12 horsepower. Though that was enough to get the Wrights' plane into the air, it was less than what many of today's riding lawn mower engines produce.

In September 1903, the Wrights returned to Kitty Hawk to fly their first powered flying machine. They had never completely assembled the plane in Dayton. Instead, they shipped the parts to North Carolina by train and put the plane together at Kill Devil Hills. Arriving at the camp they had used for the past three years, the Wrights saw that strong winds had picked up their old building and moved it closer to the water. With the help of a local man named Dan Tate, the Wright brothers soon built a new building to house the plane. The Wrights had one of their old gliders with them too, and they continued to fly it. When the wind was right, they could keep the glider aloft

WHY KITTY HAWK?

L.R.343,1899.

U. S. Department of Agriculture,
Weather Bureau.

Custom House.   Cincinnati, Ohio,   August 19,1899.

Wright Cycle Co.,

        Dayton, Ohio.

Gentlemen:
            Replying to your letter of the 16th inst.,I would say that
during September 1898,the wind at Cincinnati reached a maximum veloci-
ty of 18 miles or more on 10 days;during October 1898,on 15 days.

        In connection with kites,I would say that kite observations were
conducted by the Weather Bureau at Ft.Thomas,Ky.,during September 1898
during which month but 13 days were favorable for kite flying,on all
other days rain or light winds interfered. The style of kite used was
an improved form of the Hargrave cellular type,containing about 68
square feet of supporting surface. A steady wind of 12 miles per hour
was sufficient to lift this kite in addition to an instrument attached
to it and weighing 2.1 pounds. As to the lifting power of this style
of kite,I would say that pulls of more than 120 pounds have been recorded by the dynamometer without the kite being wrecked.
        For further information on this subject I would advise you to
write to the Weather Bureau,Instrument Division,Washington,D.C.
            Very respectfully,

                                            Local Forecast Official.

The Wrights kept the letter they received from the U.S. Weather Bureau providing information about good places to fly.

When the Wright brothers made plans to test their first glider, they wanted a spot with good weather, strong winds, and sandy beaches for soft landings. Wilbur wrote to the U.S. Weather Bureau asking for information about locations with strong, steady winds. Kitty Hawk, North Carolina, offered everything the brothers wanted. The Wrights had never heard of Kitty Hawk, but a letter from William J. Tate, the postmaster there, seemed to clinch the idea. Tate explained that the beach offered "a stretch of sandy land one mile by five, with . . . not a tree or bush anywhere to break the evenness of the wind current." Tate promised that he would do all he could to help the brothers succeed with their work. The Wrights never even visited Kitty Hawk before deciding to start their test flights there in 1900. When they arrived at the coast, it was the first time they had seen the ocean.

This new aircraft had two propellers, which would be key to getting it— and keeping it— off the ground.

for more than a minute. But the glider was no longer enough to satisfy their drive to fly through the air.

The Wrights referred to their new aircraft as simply "Flyer" or the "power machine." In some ways, it looked a lot like the old gliders. The pilot lay stretched out on his stomach on the middle of the bottom wing. From there, he could control the aircraft when it was in flight. While on the ground, the plane rested on skids, something like runners on a sled.

But the new aircraft had some key differences from the gliders of the past. Along with the engine, the two-winged aircraft also had two propellers. They

"We were expecting the most interesting results . . . and are sure that . . . we will have done something before we break camp."

would help provide thrust, or forward motion, when the plane was taking off, and then in the air. The brothers had also changed the design of the wings. In a letter to his father, Orville wrote, "It is the prettiest we have ever made, and of a much better shape."

Orville later explained that the new design made the wings both stronger and lighter than their earlier ones. And unlike the glider, the new craft would move along a wooden track laid over the sandy beach. At the end of the track, the plane would take off—if everything worked as the brothers hoped. In mid-October, Orville was confident. He wrote to a friend, "We are expecting the most interesting results . . . and are sure that, barring exasperating little accidents or some mishaps, we will have done something before we break camp."

Some mishaps did occur. During a ground test, the engine did not work properly and began to vibrate. The motion damaged the shafts that held the propellers, and they had to be shipped back to Dayton for repairs. The new shafts cracked when the brothers tested them. Orville went back to Dayton to help Charlie Taylor make another set of new shafts out of steel. Orville returned to Kitty Hawk on December 11. On December 14, the brothers were finally ready to see whether Flyer could live up to its name.

The Wright brothers were pleased with Flyer's performance during the ground test on December 14, even though it quickly crashed.

The plane weighed just over 600 pounds (270 kilograms). The brothers moved their flyer to the wooden launch track with help from John T. Daniels and two other men who worked at the nearby Kill Devil Hills Life-Saving Station. The men at these and other stations were trained to rescue sailors after shipwrecks.

A coin toss decided who would be the pilot for what the Wrights hoped would be the first successful powered air flight. Wilbur won. When the plane reached the end of the wooden track, it briefly rose into the air and then crashed down into the sand. The aircraft, though, otherwise worked as they'd hoped. Wilbur wrote home to his father that day, "There is now no question of final success."

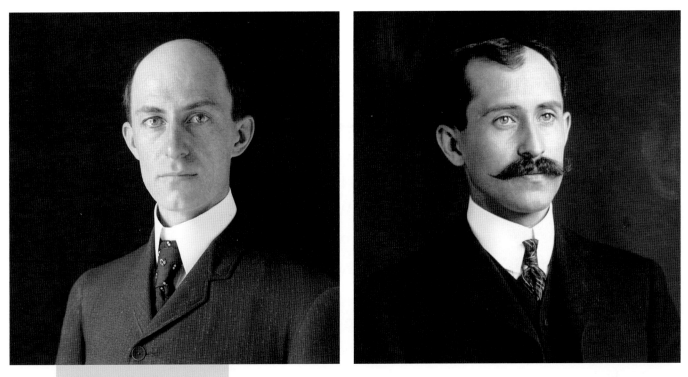

Wilbur Wright, age 38 (left), and his brother Orville, age 34, in 1905

Over the next two days, the brothers fixed minor damage to the plane. Now, on December 17, they were ready for another attempt. Daniels and two others from the station were there once again, along with two local men. This time, Orville would take the controls.

Before he climbed aboard Flyer, Orville set up a camera on a tripod near the end of the wooden launch rail. The brothers had bought their first camera several years before. They took pictures of Dayton, Ohio, their family, and friends. They photographed their gliders during their flights in North Carolina. This morning, Orville chose Daniels to be the photographer. With luck, Orville hoped to get the plane into the air for a real flight. And Daniels would snap the picture that recorded that historic moment.

ChapterTwo
BROTHERS IN BUSINESS AND INVENTION

When the Wright brothers began building and testing their first aircraft, they were not alone. In fact, Otto Lilienthal and other earlier aviators had helped inspire many inventors and engineers of the Wrights' generation. But the idea of humans flying through the air predated modern times; it went back thousands of years.

In Greek mythology, Daedalus and his son, Icarus, were held prisoner on an island. Daedalus studied how birds flew, and he decided he could create giant wings for him and his son so they could fly to freedom. They gathered bird feathers, and Daedalus used string and wax to join the feathers together and form the wings. By flapping the wings, and with help from the wind, Daedalus was able to fly. He made wings for Icarus, too, and together they planned to leave the island. Before they took off, Daedalus warned his son not to fly too high—the heat of the sun could melt the wax that held the wings together. But Icarus ignored his father. The wax melted, and he plunged to his death. Daedalus escaped safely, but after seeing his son's death, he never flew again.

By the 1500s, the idea of human flight began to move out of the realm of myths and folktales. The Italian artist and inventor Leonardo da Vinci, like

In myth, Daedalus's son, Icarus, flew too close to the sun and died as a result.

Daedalus, studied birds' wings and how they used them to fly. He was convinced people could build devices that would let them fly too. Da Vinci made hundreds of sketches based on his observation of birds. He also designed flying machines, though he never built one. One of these machines is called an *ornithopter* today. The pilot flapped its wings like a bird and used foot pedals to help the glider take off. (Centuries later, one of the artist's drawings of an ornithopter inspired comic-book artist Bob Kane to create a superhero with similar wings—Batman.)

Leonardo da Vinci made sketches of flying machines but never built one.

Da Vinci also wrote out his theories of flight. One was that birds use their wings and tail to stay balanced in flight. Achieving balance would be a key part of the Wright brothers' work. Da Vinci also understood that a person flying a glider could shift his or her weight to help stay in control of the craft. The pilots of the first practical gliders learned to do the same thing.

During the late 1700s, the French inventors Joseph and Étienne Montgolfier realized that hot air could lift a balloon off the ground. They flew a small balloon with this method in 1783. Another French inventor used hydrogen, a gas lighter than air, to send a balloon into the sky. Before the end of 1783, the Montgolfiers' balloons launched a person into the sky.

From balloons, inventors turned to creating aircraft with wings. One of the most successful was George Cayley of England. He built the first successful fixed-wing gliders in the mid-1800s. He also studied and wrote about the science of aerodynamics. His work influenced many aviators who followed him—including the Wright brothers. John Stringfellow, another British inventor of Cayley's era, created model fixed-wing planes that were powered by a small steam engine.

For Wilbur and Orville Wright, the first interest in flight came from playing with a toy. When Wilbur was 11 and Orville was 7, their father gave them a toy helicopter. The toy had two propellers and got its power from a twisted rubber band. It looked nothing like the actual helicopters that were invented during the 1900s. Those had one large spinning rotor on top and a smaller one at the rear. The large blade turned horizontally, while the smaller one spun vertically. For a time, the brothers tried to make their own copies of the flying toy that fascinated them so much.

Wilbur and Orville were part of a large family that moved several times in the boys' young lives. Wilbur was born in on April 16, 1867, in Millville, Indiana. Two years later, the Wrights moved to Dayton, Ohio,

The Wright brothers hatched many of their ideas in the house on Hawthorn Street in Dayton, Ohio, where they lived as both children and adults.

Wilbur and Orville never finished high school, but they read many of the books that filled their home.

and Orville was born there on August 19, 1871. Their father, Milton, was a minister who often moved for his work. The brothers were living in Cedar Rapids, Iowa, when they received their toy helicopter. The family moved back to Dayton for good in 1884.

Milton Wright and his wife, Susan, had a big influence on Wilbur and Orville. Milton Wright encouraged all his children to read and be curious about the world around them. Wilbur and Orville never finished high school, but they read many of the books that filled their home. Susan Wright was famous in the family for her mechanical skill. She could make toys and other items for her children. And as the brothers began tinkering, their mother saved any items they made.

Susan Wright died in 1889. The same year, 18-year-old Orville started his own business. He ran a print shop out of a shed at the Wright home. Wilbur helped him start a small newspaper that focused on events in their part of Dayton. Four years later, the brothers opened another business, selling and repairing bicycles. The so-called safety bicycle had created a cycling boom. Unlike earlier bikes, which had one huge wheel in front and a tiny one in back, the new cycle's tires were the same size. Riders used pedals attached to a chain that drove the rear wheel, just like today's bikes.

Safety bicycles eventually replaced earlier models like this, with one big wheel and one small one, which made it difficult to balance.

The bike business was good for the brothers, and in 1895 they began making and selling their own bikes. The next year, Wilbur read about the gliders of Otto Lilienthal, and he began to pursue his passion for flight in earnest. He wanted to know more about flight, so he read books about how birds flew. In 1899, Wilbur wrote the Smithsonian Institution,

Copy.

WRIGHT CYCLE COMPANY

1127 West Third Street.

Dayton, Ohio, May 30, 1899.

The Smithsonian Institution,

    Washington.

Dear Sirs:

        I have been interested in the problem of mechanical and human flight ever since as a boy I constructed a number of bats of various sizes after the style of Cayley's and Penaud's machines. My observations since have only convinced me more firmly that human flight is possible and practicable. It is only a question of knowledge and skill just as in all acrobatic feats. Birds are the most perfectly trained gymnasts in the world and are specially well fitted for their work, and it may be that man will never equal them, but no one who has watched a bird chasing an insect or another bird can doubt that feats are performed which require three or four times the effort required in ordinary flight. I believe that simple flight at least is possible to man and that the experiments and investigations of a large number of independent workers will result in the accumulation of information and knowledge and skill which will finally lead to accomplished flight.

        The works on the subject to which I have had access are Marey's and Jamieson's books published by Appleton's and various magazine and cyclopaedic articles. I am about to begin a systematic study of the subject in preparation for practical work to

The Wright brothers researched flight for years, and reached out to the Smithsonian Institution in Washington, D.C., for information.

asking for copies of all its materials relating to flight. In his letter, Wilbur said, "My observations since [childhood] have only convinced me more firmly that human flight is possible and practicable."

Among the authors both brothers read was Octave Chanute. Born in France, he spent most of his life in the United States. Chanute had written a history of aviation up to the 1890s and also built gliders. In 1900, Wilbur wrote to Chanute, explaining his and Orville's interest in flight. Chanute and the brothers became friends, and the older inventor visited the young fliers several times over the years. Although the brothers lacked much formal education, Chanute saw that they understood the science of flight.

By the time Wilbur first wrote Chanute, the Wright brothers had built and tested an aircraft of their own design. Thanks to their work in the bike shop, the brothers knew how to make small, lightweight parts. They also understood the importance of balance from their work with bicycles. Wilbur was convinced that balance, or equilibrium, would be just as important for the pilot of an aircraft. By studying aeronautics, the brothers realized that equilibrium depended on a number of factors. These included lift, the air pressure that kept an airplane up; pitch, how the plane tilted in front or back; and roll, how the plane rocked from side to side.

By also studying birds and how they moved their wings in flight, Wilbur had an idea. He believed that by controlling how a plane's wing tips moved, up or down, a pilot could keep a plane level. Twisting the wings would also let a pilot turn left or right. This twisting was later called wing warping.

The brothers tested all these ideas with their first glider. It was really more of a kite, with two wings,

Wilbur was convinced that balance, or equilibrium, would be just as important for the pilot of an aircraft.

A TEACHER AND SUPPORTER

An assistant flew one of Octave Chanute's biplane gliders, which had two wings stacked one above the other. Chanute and his designs were helpful to the Wrights in their flight experiments.

Octave Chanute (1832–1910) played a key role in helping humans take to the skies. Born in France, Chanute had come to the United States as a child. He became an engineer and helped design railways and bridges before developing an interest in flight. In 1894, he published *Progress in Flying Machines*, which looked at the recent history of the effort to build aircraft. It was one of the books Wilbur received from the Smithsonian Institution. Chanute also tried to share the ideas of the inventors working in aviation at the time.

He wanted anyone interested in flight to have access to the latest knowledge. Starting in 1896, Chanute designed and built several of his own gliders. He was too old to fly the gliders himself, but an assistant successfully flew them on the sand dunes along Lake Michigan. The Wrights used Chanute's biplane design for their own gliders. After meeting the Wright brothers, Chanute encouraged their efforts. He also photographed some of the brothers' glider flights at Kill Devil Hills.

5 feet (1.5 meters) long. The wings had a wooden frame covered with fabric. Cords attached to the wings let the brothers control them from the ground. The test flight showed that Wilbur's ideas were right. He had found the way to keep a plane balanced and make it turn. The Wrights began designing a glider that would be large enough to carry a pilot. Like the kite, it had a biplane wing design.

Since their days in the newspaper business, the brothers worked hard on whatever project they pursued. Their work was their life. Neither man married, and they remained in the family home in Dayton. With most of their interests, the brothers were self-taught. That was true, too, of one of their favorite hobbies—photography. The brothers learned how to develop the images and make prints of the scenes they photographed. Orville kept detailed records of where and when he took each picture. He also noted technical data, such as the f-stop setting, which controlled how much light entered the camera.

One of the brothers' earliest pictures shows a train wreck that took place in Dayton in 1897. Two trains had collided. One of the survivors of the crash was their father, Milton Wright. Over the next few years, the brothers took pictures of a severe flood that hit Dayton, as well as of neighbors, relatives, and scenes from their bike shop. Photography soon became more than a hobby, as the brothers sold

Their work was their life. Neither man married, and they remained in the family home in Dayton.

The Wright brothers' love of photography would later bring proof of their flight to the world. But in 1897, one of their earliest photographs was of a terrible train wreck near their home.

supplies to other photographers. They also used their camera to record the progress of their work to build aircraft.

In 1900, the Wrights built their first aircraft large enough to carry a person. In September, they made their first trip to Kitty Hawk to test this new glider. At first they flew it as a kite, controlling it from the ground. Then the brothers flew it as a glider. The pilot controlled the wing warp by pulling cables attached to the wings.

PHOTOGRAPHY IN THE 1890S

Early cameras were so heavy that they were mostly carried and used by men. The new Eastman-Kodak cameras were advertised as light enough to be used by women.

The first cameras appeared in the 1820s. They used silver plates coated with chemicals to capture images, when the plates were aimed at a subject and exposed to light. For most of the 1800s, cameras used this process, though glass plates replaced the silver ones. Improved mixtures of chemicals helped make the images clearer and required less light. In 1888, George Eastman helped make photography easier when he introduced film cameras. The chemicals were applied to frames of rolls of film, which replaced the glass plates.

The Eastman Kodak Company produced cameras that were smaller and easier to use than the plate cameras. Amateur photographers using Kodak did not even have to develop their own pictures—they sent the film to Eastman's company. Despite the growing popularity of film cameras, when the Wright brothers bought their first camera, it used glass plates. Each plate was 5 inches (13 centimeters) wide by 4 inches (10 cm) high. Records show that the brothers took their first photo with the camera on October 20, 1897.

For these flights, the glider was brought to a sand hill. Orville and postmaster Tate each held on to the end of the wings. Wilbur also helped carry the aircraft, then jumped on board right before the other two men let go of the wings. The aircraft began to glide through the air.

These piloted flights were not what the Wrights expected. The glider could not generate enough lift. As a result, most of the tests that year involved flying the glider as a kite, with no one on board. The brothers also took pictures of their own aircraft—including the wreckage that resulted from early crashes.

Despite early mishaps, the brothers did manage to make some successful piloted flights. On one, the

The Wright brothers had a lot of failures before they had success—and they photographed those too.

glider reached a speed of 30 miles (48 km) per hour as it came in for a landing.

When not working on the glider, the Wrights spent time on the beach studying the flights of birds. Daniels, from the Life-Saving Station, later said that he and others at the station watched the Wrights use their arms to imitate the birds. Daniels said, "We couldn't help thinking they were just a pair of poor nuts . . . they were crazy, but we just had to admire the way they could move their arms this way and that and bend their elbows and wrist bones up and down and which a way, just like the [birds] moved their wings."

The brothers returned to North Carolina the next year with a larger glider—the largest ever flown at that time. Wilbur flew the aircraft, but once again the glider did not create as much lift as the brothers expected. Still, Wilbur managed flights up to 350 ft. (105 m) long. At one point, the glider reached a height of about 40 ft. (10 m), but usually it flew close to the ground. Chanute, who had come to visit at Kitty Hawk, said they were the longest flights ever recorded. But the brothers were discouraged for a time. Wilbur later said, "We doubted that we would resume our experiments."

Still, despite the challenges, Wilbur and Orville had not lost the desire to explore human flight. Back in Dayton, they built a wind tunnel—a device that

"We couldn't help thinking they were just a pair of poor nuts . . . ."

The brothers kept trying to fly, fixing problems and improving gliders after each flight.

would let them see how different wing designs worked without actually building and flying an entire aircraft. The "tunnel" was simply a long, wooden box that was open at both ends. A fan created the wind. From these experiments, they improved their glider. Also, that fall Wilbur gave a speech in Chicago about aeronautics and the brothers' glider experiments. He used some of their photos from Kitty Hawk to illustrate his talk.

In 1902, the brothers returned to Kitty Hawk for test flights of their new glider. The aircraft now had wings that were 32 ft. (9.8 m) long. This glider was much easier to control and flew much better than previous models. The brothers made hundreds of flights that fall. Before returning home, they knew they were ready for the next step—to equip their aircraft with an engine. Then, when they returned to North Carolina in 1903, they would try to make history.

ChapterThree
MAKING HISTORY

Back at Kitty Hawk in 1903, the Wright Brothers' first powered flight was delayed as they dealt with assembling their plane and getting the propeller fixed. That fall, the Wrights also encountered fierce storms. During one, the winds reached 75 mi. (120 km) per hour. They began to tear off the tar-paper roof on the building the brothers used as a workshop and hangar. Orville went out in the storm to try to fix the roof, using hammer and nails. Wilbur went along to help. As he later described the scene, Wilbur joked that the wind was so strong that his brother more often than not "hit the roof or his fingers instead of the nail." But he got the job done, and both brothers "rushed for cover."

On the afternoon of December 14, the brothers were finally ready to try to fly. They sent a message to the Life-Saving Station asking for help. With the aid of John T. Daniels and the other men who came, the brothers brought their plane up a 150-ft. (45-m) incline. Then they laid down a track, 60 ft. (18 m) long. The plane would slide along this track before taking off. When they fired up the engine, some local boys watching the Wrights work heard the noise and ran away in fright.

With Wilbur at the controls, Orville ran alongside the plane, steadying the wing. He ran until the plane was going too fast for him, then

Men from the Life-Saving Station (with a dog and two boys following along) helped move the Wright brothers' plane to the hill from which they would attempt lift-off.

watched Flyer briefly rise about 15 ft. (4.5 m) and travel 60 ft. (18 m) from the end of the track before crashing down. Wilbur called it an easy landing, but he blamed himself for not keeping the plane in the air. A picture taken after the failed flight shows him lying down at the controls. The photographer is unknown, but his shadow as he stands behind the camera is visible in the bottom of the photo. During this trial, a few pieces on the plane broke, so the brothers spent the next two days repairing them. On December 17, they were ready to try again.

It was a cold day at Kill Devil Hills. The wind was stronger than on the 14th, maybe too strong. Keeping the plane balanced would be tricky. Daniels and some other lifesavers and local men came down from the Life-Saving Station to help. He and the others took their job seriously, and Daniels later remembered that none of them felt like talking. His most important task that day would be taking a picture if Flyer got airborne. He was an unlikely photographer to take such an important photo. Daniels had never taken a picture before. By some reports, he'd never even seen a camera before.

By now, the brothers had bought a larger, more expensive camera than their first one. Their Korona-V camera, made in Rochester, New York, used glass plates that were 5 inches (13 cm) by 7 inches (18 cm) long. It was easy to use, once set in its tripod. All Daniels had to do was squeeze a rubber bulb attached to the camera. When he squeezed it, the camera's shutter would open and take the picture.

At 10:35 a.m., with Orville as pilot, Flyer began to cruise down the launch track. This time, the track was on level ground. As Orville had done on the first try, Wilbur held onto the wing and ran alongside the plane. He was able to keep up with it all along the

> Daniels had never taken a picture before. By some reports, he'd never even seen a camera before.

A FAILED ATTEMPT

Samuel Langley spent a lot of money and time developing his biplane. Sadly, the launch attempt ended quickly when the plane immediately crashed into the river.

During 1903, while the Wright brothers were preparing for their first powered flight, another inventor was hoping he would make aviation history. Samuel Langley was the head of the Smithsonian Institution. He had a background in science and math, and by the 1890s he had learned all he could about aeronautics. Langley decided that a powered aircraft could fly with a steam engine, and he built several successful model planes. He called these model planes aerodromes. Langley was helped by the U.S. government, which gave him $50,000 to develop his aircraft. By August 1903, he was ready to test a larger version. By now, he was powering his plane with a gas engine. Flying without a pilot, the new aerodrome was launched with a catapult from a houseboat in the Potomac River, about 30 mi. (50 km) south of Washington, D.C. The aerodrome flew for about 1,000 ft. (305 m) before crashing into the river. In October, Langley and his assistants returned to the Potomac. This time, a pilot named Charles Manly would try to fly a full-sized version of the aerodrome. But the plane crashed into the river as soon as it left the catapult. In December, just days before the Wrights first tried to launch Flyer, Langley and Manly tried the aerodrome one more time. Once again, the plane never took off, and Langley stopped his work on airplanes. The plane was preserved, and in 1914 it finally flew, with adjustments made by another aviation pioneer, Glenn Curtiss.

track. Then Flyer and Orville rose off the ground. For 12 seconds, the aircraft stayed in the air, covering 120 ft. (37 m). The Wrights had decided to keep the plane close to the ground, in case it crashed. It flew at an altitude of about 10 ft. (3 m). Then, one wing dipped into the sand, and Flyer came down.

The brothers would have to wait until they returned to Dayton to see if Daniels had captured the historic flight. But they already knew they had done something important. Though their plane had not gone far, the Wright brothers had shown that a plane equipped with a motor and carrying a person could take off from the ground and fly.

The brothers followed that flight with three more that day, as they took turns at the controls.

The Wright brothers took photos of some of their flights on December 17, including this, the third of four flights that day.

THE UNLIKELY PHOTOGRAPHER

John T. Daniels (left), who took the photograph of the Wright brothers' first successful flight, placed a wreath at their memorial many years later.

North Carolina native John T. Daniels was 30 years old when he took the famous picture that made him part of history. Daniels was a member of the Life-Saving Service. The U.S. government created the service in 1878, though it had already built some life-saving stations along the East Coast. In 1915, the service would become part of the U.S. Coast Guard. Daniels and the men he worked with kept watch over a 4-mile (6-km) stretch of beach around Kill Devil Hills. The "surfmen," as they were called, grew friendly with the Wright brothers as they did their flying tests at Kitty Hawk. When the brothers needed the surfmen's help, they flew a red flag that Daniels and the others could see from their station. When the time came for Daniels to take the picture of the first flight, he was so excited that he almost forgot to squeeze the camera's bulb.

After the fourth flight of the day, Daniels was holding onto Flyer when a strong gust of wind picked up the plane. As Daniels later described it, the wind "swept it across the beach just like you've seen an umbrella turned inside out and loose in the wind." Daniels got tangled up in the wire that held some of the plane together and bounced along with it as the wind carried the plane across the beach. Daniels said, "When the thing did stop for half a second I nearly broke up every wire and upright getting out of it." Orville Wright wrote in his diary, "His escape was miraculous."

Daniels got some bruises and scratches and he said, "I . . . was so scared I couldn't walk straight for a few minutes." Years later, he would say that he survived the world's first airplane crash. Daniels kept a piece of the wood that broke off the plane, and he sometimes gave bits of it to visitors as a souvenir. Daniels also attended some of the ceremonies held at Kill Devil Hills to mark the first flight. He died on January 31, 1948, one day after Orville Wright's death.

The brothers didn't photograph the second flight, but on the third, Wilbur took a picture of Orville as he traveled about 175 ft. (50 m). On the last try, Wilbur managed to cover about 850 ft. (260 m) on a flight that lasted just under a minute. A gust of wind caused the plane to go down. Orville or someone else took a picture of the last flight and of Flyer on the ground.

That afternoon, the brothers sent a telegram to their father in Dayton. The first word of the message was "Success." Then, Orville briefly described the flights, noting Flyer had achieved an average speed of 31 mi. (50 km) per hour. He ended by saying the brothers would be home for Christmas.

But before they returned home, word of their first flights reached the newspapers. Their brother Lorin

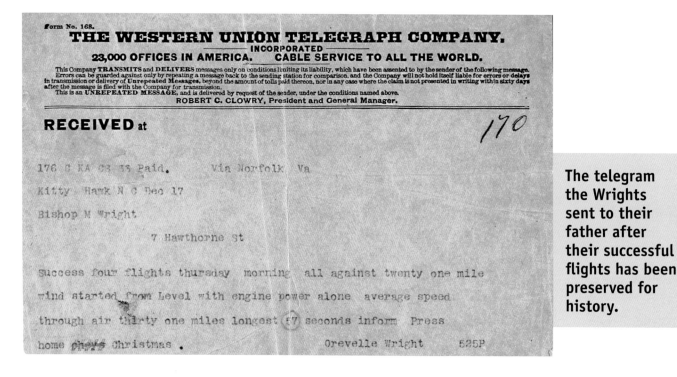

The telegram the Wrights sent to their father after their successful flights has been preserved for history.

told it to one Dayton newspaper, which was also a member of the Associated Press. This company shares news and photos with papers all over the country. The editor at the paper, however, was not impressed with the brothers' achievement. Another Dayton paper did run a brief article. Most of the news about the historic flight came from a Virginia newspaper, which had gotten its information from

A Virginia newspaper reported many inaccurate facts in its story about the Wright brothers' successful flight.

the company that transmitted the Wrights' telegram home. That news, however, was mostly wrong. The Virginia paper said the brothers had flown 3 mi. (4.8 km), soaring over the ocean as well as the beach. Still, that first article provided most of the information anyone knew about the flights, aside from the seven men who had been there.

Back at their photography studio in Dayton, the brothers didn't know what they would see on the glass plates used in their camera at Kill Devil Hills. As Wilbur had written in 1901, "We pass moments of as thrilling interest as any in the field, when the image begins to appear on the plate and it is yet an open question whether we have a picture of a flying machine, or merely a patch of open sky." Orville developed the picture that Daniels had taken of the first flight. It clearly showed a flying machine, and not a patch of open sky.

In the photo, the plane is in the air after beginning on the launching track. At this point, Flyer had been in the air just a few seconds. Wilbur stands to the right, after having let go of the wing. On the ground are some of the tools the brothers used to prepare the plane for flight. The image also shows footprints in the soft North Carolina sand. But the public would not see the picture, at least not right away.

The brothers wanted to keep details about their aircraft to themselves. Wilbur wrote to Chanute

The Wright brothers did not release the historic photo that proved their flight for several years. The lack of evidence led some people to doubt that they'd succeeded.

on December 28, "We are giving no pictures nor descriptions of machine or methods at present." In 1908, *The Century Magazine* published an article written by the Wright brothers. It was, the magazine said, "the first popular account of their experiments prepared by the inventors." The story included the image of the historic first flight—the first time it was published. It had taken five years for Daniels' picture to reach the public. But even then, the photo was not widely seen, since *The Century* reached a fairly small audience.

Despite wanting at first to keep information about Flyer to themselves, the brothers realized they needed to say something about their flights. They wanted to correct the errors that had been spread around the country, based on the newspaper article from Virginia. So, early in January 1904, the brothers wrote a public statement, which they gave to the Associated Press. They corrected the mistakes about the details of their flights. But they did not describe Flyer. The statement said, "From the beginning we have employed entirely new principles of control; and as all the experiments have been conducted at our own expense without assistance from any individual or institution we do not feel ready at present to give out any pictures or detailed description of the machine."

So, as 1904 began, the brothers returned to their bicycle shop and made plans for a bigger and better plane. The Wrights' Flyer would never fly again.

ChapterFour
HEROES OF AVIATION

As the Wright brothers began to work on the Flyer II, they decided they could no longer afford to travel to North Carolina for their test flights. Instead, they found a field outside of Dayton where they could fly. The field was called Huffman Prairie, and it was not an isolated spot, like Kill Devil Hills. A trolley traveled by the field, so the brothers' activity would not be private. And instead of having miles of sand, the field had trees and fences around its sides. Huffman Prairie was a spot where horses and cows grazed. Before the brothers launched a plane, they would have to clear the animals from the pasture.

Back in Dayton, Charlie Taylor built a more powerful engine, while the brothers designed and built their new plane. Their goal was to make it not only bigger, but stronger than the original Flyer. In May 1904, they were ready to test it at Huffman Prairie. This time, they invited reporters to witness the flights. At first, bad weather kept the new plane on the ground. On May 26, when Flyer II finally got airborne, it only traveled 25 ft. (7.6 m). On June 10, Wilbur noted in a letter to his father that they "made a blunder in steering just after the start and hit the ground after going about 60 feet." The brothers had

Wilbur and Orville worked on their second powered machine in Ohio, in a field not far from their home.

their camera with them on some if not all of the trips to Huffman Prairie, though only a few of these glass plates survived. A picture taken in May shows both brothers by their plane. One of the pictures from that summer shows Flyer II on the ground, resting on the launching track. Others show the plane in the air.

The brothers came up with a new way to help get their plane off the ground. They built their version of a catapult to help speed the plane down the track. It consisted of four wooden poles set in a square, leaning toward the center so the tops touched. It looked like the oil rigs used to pump oil out of the ground. The catapult used ropes, pulleys, and pieces of metal that weighed as much as 1,600 lbs. (725 kg). Dropping the weights from the top of

At Huffman Prairie, they were able to stay in the air even longer, and fly even farther, than at Kill Devil Hills.

the rig pulled Flyer II along the track. The device gave the plane a faster launch speed than the engine alone could manage. By now, the Wrights were also able to safely land their plane after its flights.

In September, using the catapult, Wilbur took off on a flight that covered more than 2,500 ft. (760 m). On another flight of just over 4,000 ft. (1,220 m), he made a complete circle in midair—a first for the Wrights. On November 9, Wilbur made four complete turns around the field, covering a total distance of almost 3 mi. (5 km), while staying aloft for just over 5 minutes. Pictures the brothers took that day and the following week were published four years later in *The Century Magazine*. They appeared in the same article that included the Daniels photo of the first flight. On a flight in December, Orville covered about the same distance as Wilbur had the previous month. On these flights, the plane was flying at about 38 mi. (60 km) per hour.

On December 20, Wilbur wrote to Chanute that the brothers were stopping their flights for the year. They had made a total of 105 flights in 1904. But even when not out in Huffman Prairie, the brothers were busy. In January 1905, they wrote a letter to the U.S. War Department describing their success and suggesting that their plane could be useful in wartime. Officers could use it to send messages or scout out enemy positions. But the government was not interested in their invention. Its response suggested that the officials in the War Department had not really read the Wrights' letter, or they didn't understand it. A major general wrote that "it appears . . . that their machine has not yet been brought to the stage of practical operation." But the Wrights had clearly stated that they had flown a plane that "not only flies through the air at high speed, but it also lands without being wrecked." They also described some of the more than 100 flights made during 1904.

The British government, however, was interested in the plane. And in France, several inventors had spent 1904 working on gliders based on the Wrights' design. That October, a French aeronautics club offered money to anyone who could fly certain

" . . . these
flights have
been made
by some
newspapers
the subject
of a great
'mystery.'"

distances. The biggest prize would go to the person who made a circular flight that covered a little more than a half-mile. The Wrights had already done this and more in a powered airplane in America.

Throughout early 1905, the brothers worked on Flyer III. It included, once again, a more powerful engine and some design changes that would make the aircraft easier to control. By this time, the Wrights had a building at Huffman Prairie, and in May they began assembling the new plane there. Through the year, they made 50 flights. On one of these flights, Orville completed the first known figure-eight maneuver in an aircraft.

The best flights came in September and October. On October 5, Wilbur stayed in the air for 38 minutes and covered 24 mi. (39 km), the longest flight so far. He landed only because he had run out of gas.

The Wrights' family and friends came out to watch some of the flights. So did some reporters. Given that the flights were public, the brothers wrote several years later that they were surprised that "these flights have been made by some newspapers the subject of a great 'mystery.'"

The Wrights also took their trusty Korona-V camera with them to Huffman Prairie. One of the images captured that year was taken just before the first flight of 1905, with Orville as pilot. The catapult is also visible. Others showed Flyer III in the air

In the last photo of 1905 flights, Orville again flew Flyer II.

during the long September and October flights. Twelve shots were taken of the September 29 flight. The last picture of the year was taken on October 4.

The test flights for 1905 ended soon after that. Just days before the last flight, the brothers wrote again to the U.S. War Department about their plane. Wilbur was convinced that their work in 1905 proved that airplanes were now practical enough to be used to carry supplies or go on scouting missions.

The brothers wanted to give their own government one more chance to buy their invention. They also offered to build a new plane that could carry more than one person. Once again, the government was not interested. The reply did say that the brothers would have to turn over the written designs of their plane to the government before the War Department took any action. The brothers were not willing to share their secrets for achieving human flight.

By the end of the year, the French government showed the most interest in Flyer III. The brothers signed a contract to build the French a similar plane. French inventors were still actively trying to build their own plane, turning from gliders to powered aircraft. But it would take until September 1906 for a French flyer to cover just over 700 ft. (210 m). No one was close to building a plane that could cover the distances Flyer III did.

To some French, though, the Wrights' success seemed too hard to believe. In 1906, one newspaper suggested the brothers might be liars, not fliers. In March of that year, representatives from France came to Dayton to meet with the Wrights. The French wanted to discuss their contract with the brothers and to see the plane. The brothers showed them some of their photos instead and let them hear the reports of people who had seen the plane in flight.

WERE THE WRIGHTS REALLY FIRST?

Gustave Whitehead sits on the ground next to his flying machine in 1902. There's no proof that it actually flew.

In August 1901, a newspaper in Bridgeport, Connecticut, reported that a German immigrant named Gustave Whitehead had built a flying machine that covered a half-mile. Other newspapers soon picked up the story. Whitehead later said that he made two more flights in 1902, which would mean that he, not the Wright brothers, was the inventor of the first powered aircraft. Since the 1930s, a small number of people have supported Whitehead's claim. Most aviation experts, however, have rejected it. The original news story quoted a supposed eyewitness to the Connecticut flight.

But years later, the witness said he did not see a flight and never heard that Whitehead ever flew any of the aircraft he built. One of the people who gave Whitehead money for his work also doubted Whitehead ever achieved flight. And another man who worked with Whitehead said he was "a supreme master of the art of lying." Yet in the 2000s, some people still believe that Whitehead beat the Wrights into the air. That has led both the Smithsonian Institution and *Scientific American*, among others, to assert over and over that the Wrights were the ones who made history.

The brothers spent much of 1906 working on a new engine. They were also focused on building new planes that they could sell. An important moment came in May, when the Wrights received a patent for their invention. The U.S. government had recognized that the Wright glider of 1902 used a completely new design to achieve flight. That design was also used for Flyer and the planes that followed it. With the patent, no one else could use the Wrights' design for an airplane without their permission.

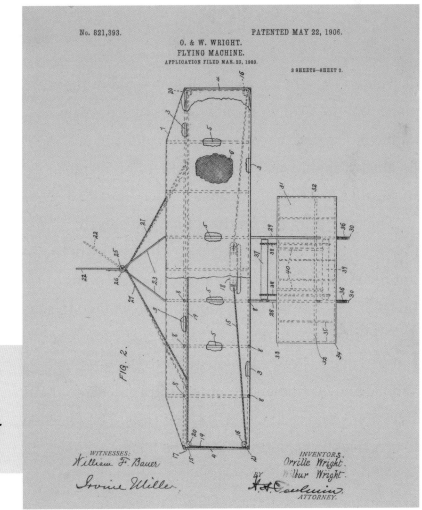

The Wrights patented their airplane a few years after their first flight.

Even with the patent, the Wrights' photos, and all the reports from eyewitnesses, some people still refused to believe the Wrights had flown a powered aircraft. *Scientific American*, a respected U.S. journal, wrote in January 1906 about the brothers' "alleged experiments." The magazine ignored all the reports that were readily available. A few months later, after contacting some of the eyewitnesses and getting their reports, the magazine finally admitted that the Wrights had done what they said they'd done.

In 1907, the brothers traveled to Europe, still trying to sell their planes. They went to France and Germany. The French were still interested in the plane, but the deal with the brothers was uncertain. While in France, they saw a French plane in action. Its longest flight was just a half-mile. The Wrights were still the kings of aviation.

The next year, the brothers finally received interest from the U.S. government to buy one of the improved Flyer III planes. The French deal went through, too, but the government there wanted to see one of the planes in action. The Wrights had already shipped one to France. To prepare for the tests, Wilbur and Orville made some improvements to their 1905 plane and took it to Kill Devil Hills. They needed to practice their piloting skills. The business concerns of selling the plane had kept both brothers on the ground for more than two years. The new model

"We are
children
compared
to the
Wrights."

allowed the pilot to sit up while flying. During these flights, a photographer for *Collier's Weekly* magazine took a picture that became the first published photo of a Wright plane in the air. John T. Daniels's historic picture and others the Wrights took finally appeared in print later in the year. Another first came in North Carolina when Wilbur carried the first passenger.

After the time in North Carolina, Wilbur headed to Le Mans, France. On August 8, 1908, he dazzled a crowd there with what was, for the Wrights, a short flight—just 2 mi. (3.2 km). But French pilots who watched him effortlessly make full circles knew they had seen something special. One said, "We are children compared to the Wrights." As news of the plane spread, more than 2,000 people turned out for the next flights. On one, Wilbur made two figure-eights, then landed at the exact spot where he had taken off. There was no doubt now in France that the Wrights were fliers and not liars.

Since almost no one had ever flown before, the brothers tried to describe the experience in their 1908 article for *The Century Magazine.* "The ground under you is at first a perfect blur, but as you rise the objects become clearer. At a height of one hundred feet you feel hardly any motion at all, except for the wind which strikes your face. If you did not take the precaution to fasten your hat before starting, you have probably lost it by this time. . . . Although

Le Petit Journal

Le Petit Journal   5 CENTIMES   SUPPLEMENT ILLUSTRÉ   5 CENTIMES   ABONNEMENTS

CHAQUE JOUR — 6 PAGES — 5 CENTIMES   Le Petit Journal agricole, 5 cent. — La Mode du Petit Journal, 10 cent.

Administration : 61, rue Lafayette   Le Petit Journal illustré de la Jeunesse, 10 cent.

Les manuscrits ne sont pas rendus   On s'abonne sans frais dans tous les bureaux de poste

Dix-neuvième Année   DIMANCHE 30 AOUT 1908   Numéro 928

L'AEROPLANE DE WILBUR WRIGHT EN PLEIN VOL.

The Wright brothers' flights got more publicity in France than in the United States.

the machine often lands when traveling at a speed of a mile a minute, you feel no shock whatever. . . . The motor close beside you kept up an almost deafening roar during the whole flight, yet in your excitement, you did not notice it till it stopped!"

With the plane a proven success, the Wrights

started a new company that focused solely on aviation. They opened a school to train pilots, and they made money by making flights in front of awed crowds. They also had their contracts with the U.S. and foreign governments. With all their business deals, the brothers became wealthy.

In 1910, the Wrights made some personal history. On a flight at Huffman Prairie, Wilbur and Orville flew together for the first time. It would also be their only flight together. In 1912, Wilbur developed typhoid fever. Medicines that cure this illness were not available then, and in May, Wilbur died. He was 45 years old. At the church service before he was buried, about 25,000 people came to pay their respects.

Orville lived much longer than his brother. He died in 1948 at the age of 77. He saw how the pioneering plane he and Wilbur had built led to planes suitable for military use, just as they thought it would. It also led to planes powered by jet engines and able to carry dozens of passengers across the oceans.

Seeing the picture John T. Daniels took at Kill Devil Hills in 1903, it would be hard to imagine the future developments in flight. The picture, though, has become almost as famous as the men who built the plane. It has been printed in countless books and magazines about the Wrights and the history of aviation. It also served as the model for the image on the back of the North Carolina state quarter, which was released in 2001. The original

The Wright brothers lived together their whole lives. Orville (right) lived 36 years longer than Wilbur.

glass plate used in 1903 is part of a collection of 303 Wright brothers' plates that were donated to the Library of Congress in Washington, D.C. Those pictures help document the efforts of two self-taught inventors who made history.

THE CENTENNIAL STATUES

The 100th anniversary statue of the Wright brothers' first flight memorializes both the flight—and the moment when the photo was taken.

In 2003, to mark the centennial, or 100th anniversary, of the Wright brothers' first powered flight, the state of North Carolina put up a statue at Kill Devil Hills. It shows a life-size version of Flyer, made from stainless steel, just before it leaves the ground. The sculpture also shows the Wright brothers by the plane, and John T. Daniels standing behind the tripod that held the camera he used to take his famous photo. In 2005, statues of the four other men who were there that day—Adam Etheridge, Will Dough, W.C. Brinkley, and Johnny Moore—were added to the site.

Timeline

1867

Wilbur Wright is born on April 16 in Millville, Indiana.

1871

Orville Wright is born on August 19 in Dayton, Ohio.

1897

The brothers buy their first camera and soon begin selling photographic supplies in their shop.

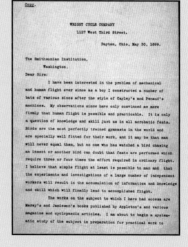

1899

Wilbur writes to the Smithsonian Institution, asking for its materials on flight.

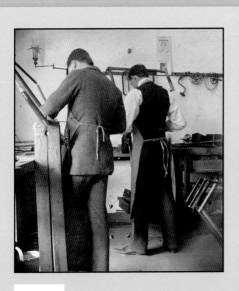

1893

The Wright brothers open a bicycle shop in Dayton.

1896

Otto Lilienthal dies after crashing one of his gliders. Wilbur reads about him and becomes interested in flight.

1900

The Wrights make their first trip to North Carolina to test their first glider large enough to carry a person.

1903

On December 17, the brothers fly their first plane equipped with an engine. John T. Daniels takes a photograph of the first flight.

Timeline

1904

The brothers fly a new and improved plane at Huffman Prairie, near Dayton. They continue to take pictures of their plane in flight.

1909

The Wright Company is established to manufacture airplanes.

1912

Wilbur Wright dies on May 30.

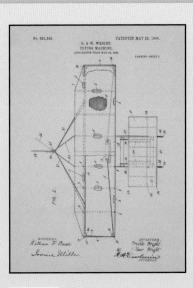

1906

The Wrights receive a patent for their 1902 glider, which inspired their engine-powered aircraft.

1908

Wilbur impresses large crowds in France with the brothers' improved aircraft. Daniels' photo of 1903's successful powered flight is finally published.

1948

Orville Wright dies on January 30.

2003

For the centennial of the first powered flight, the state of North Carolina erects a statue at Kill Devil Hills, showing the Wright brothers, their plane, and Daniels taking a historic photograph of that flight.

Glossary

aerodynamics—a branch of science that deals with the motion of air and the forces that affect objects moving through it

aeronautics—the science dealing with the flying of aircraft

aviators—people who pilot aircraft

biplane—an airplane with two wings on each side, placed one above the other

catapult—a device that propels objects into the air

f-stop—part of a camera that determines how much light enters through the lens

hangar—a place where airplanes are repaired and stored

internal combustion—referring to a kind of engine that burns a mixture of fuel and air in small chambers called cylinders

lift—the force that keeps an airplane in the air

ornithopter—an aircraft that gets its chief support and flight from flapping wings

patent—a legal document giving an inventor sole rights to make and sell an item he or she invented

pitch—the up and down motion of the front of a plane while in flight

roll—the up and down motion of the wings of a plane while in flight

shutter—the part of a camera that opens to let light in

thrust—the force required to move an airplane forward

Additional Resources

Books

Beevor, Lucy. *The Invention of the Airplane*. North Mankato, MN: Capstone Press, 2018.

Goldstone, Lawrence. *Higher, Steeper, Faster: The Daredevils Who Conquered the Skies*. New York: Little, Brown and Company, 2017.

Hagler, Gina. *Orville and Wilbur Wright: The Brothers Who Invented the Airplane*. New York: Enslow Publishing, 2020.

Kenney, Karen Latchana. *Who Invented the Airplane?: Wright Brothers vs. Whitehead*. Minneapolis: Lerner Publications, 2018.

Tise, Larry E. *Circa 1903: North Carolina's Outer Banks at the Dawn of Flight*. Chapel Hill: University of North Carolina Press, 2019.

_____. *Conquering the Sky: The Secret Flights of the Wright Brothers at Kitty Hawk*. New York: Palgrave Macmillan, 2009.

_____. *Hidden Images of the Wright Brothers at Kitty Hawk*. Charleston, SC: History Press, 2019.

Websites

History of Flight
https://www.grc.nasa.gov/WWW/k-12/UEET/StudentSite/historyofflight.html

The Wright Brothers: The Invention of the Aerial Age
https://airandspace.si.edu/exhibitions/wright-brothers/online/index.cfm

Wright Brothers Negatives
https://www.loc.gov/collections/wright-brothers-negatives/about-this-collection/

Critical Thinking Questions

If you were the Wright brothers, would you have released the photos of your historic flight right away? Why or why not?

The Wright brothers worked on bicycles before they turned to the creation of aircraft. Name a few ways in which working on bicycles may have helped them when they began to build a flyer.

John T. Daniels had never taken a photograph before the Wright brothers' famous flight. Do you think the photo's reception might've been different if a professional photographer had taken the shot? Why or why not?

Source Notes

p. 4, "From the time we were little children…" Marvin W. McFarland, ed. *The Papers of Wilbur and Orville Wright: Including the Chanute-Wright Letters and Other Papers of Octave Chanute*. New York: McGraw-Hill, 1953, volume 1, p. iv.

p. 6, "Lilienthal not only thought…" Ibid., p. 101.

p. 9, "A stretch of sandy land…" David McCullough. *The Wright Brothers*. New York: Simon & Schuster, 2015, p. 41.

p. 10, "power machine…" Orville Wright. *How We Invented the Airplane: An Illustrated History*. Fred C. Kelly, ed., New York: Dover Publications, 1988, p. 20.

p. 11, "We are expecting the most interesting results…" *The Papers of Wilbur and Orville Wright*, volume 1, p. 364.

p. 12, "There is now no question of final success." Ibid., p. 393.

p. 21, "My observations since childhood…" Ibid., p. 4.

p. 28, "We couldn't help thinking…" John T. Daniels, interview with *Collier's Weekly*, September 17, 1927, Smithsonian Education, http://www.smithsonianeducation.org/educators/lesson_plans/wright/group_d.html Accessed on August 30, 2019.

p. 28, "We doubted that we would resume our experiments…" Tom D. Crouch. *Wings: A History of Aviation from Kites to the Space Age*. New York: W.W. Norton, 2003, p. 64.

p. 30, "Hit the roof or his fingers…rushed for cover…" *The Papers of Wilbur and Orville Wright*, volume 1, p. 367.

p. 35, "Swept it across the beach…" Daniels' interview with *Collier's Weekly*.

p. 35, "His escape was miraculous…" *The Papers of Wilbur and Orville Wright*, volume 1, p. 397.

p. 35, "I…was so scared…" Daniels interview with *Collier's Weekly*.

p. 36, "Success…" *The Papers of Wilbur and Orville Wright*, volume 1, p. 397.

p. 38, "We pass moments of thrilling interest…" Ibid., p. 116.

p. 39, "We are giving no pictures…" Ibid., p. 401.

p. 39, "The first popular account…" Wilbur Wright and Orville Wright, "The Wright Brothers Aeroplane," *Century Magazine*, 76, no. 5, September 1908, p. 641.

p. 40, "From the beginning we have employed…" *The Papers of Wilbur and Orville Wright*, volume 1, p. 411.

p. 40, "Made a blunder in steering…" Ibid., p. 439.

p. 44, "It appears…" *How We Invented the Airplane*, p. 52.

p. 44, "Not only flies through the air…" *The Wright Brothers*, p. 123.

p. 45, "These flights have been made…" "The Wright Brothers Aeroplane," p. 650.

p. 48, "Supreme master of the art of lying…" Tom D. Crouch, "Air and Space Curator: The Wright Brothers Were Most Definitely the First in Flight," Smithsonian.com, March 18, 2013, https://www.smithsonianmag.com/smithsonian-institution/air-and-space-curator-the-wright-brothers-were-most-definitely-the-first-in-flight-3903093,Accessed on September 12, 2019.

p. 50, "Alleged experiments…" *The Papers of Wilbur and Orville Wright*, volume 2, p. 694.

p. 51, "We are children compared to the Wrights…" *The Wright Brothers*, p. 171.

p. 51, "The ground under you is at first a perfect blur…" "The Wright Brothers Aeroplane," p. 650.

Select Bibliography

Books

Crouch, Tom D. *Wings: A History of Aviation from Kites to the Space Age*. New York: W.W. Norton, 2003.

McCullough, David. *The Wright Brothers*. New York: Simon & Schuster, 2015.

McFarland, Marvin W., ed. *The Papers of Wilbur and Orville Wright: Including the Chanute-Wright Letters and Other Papers of Octave Chanute*. Two volumes. New York: McGraw-Hill, 1953.

Wright, Orville. *How We Invented the Airplane: An Illustrated History*. Fred C. Kelly, ed. New York: Dover Publications, 1988.

Websites and Articles

Crouch, Tom D., "Air and Space Curator: The Wright Brothers Were Most Definitely the First in Flight," Smithsonian.com, March 18, 2013, https://www.smithsonianmag.com/smithsonian-institution/air-and-space-curator-the-wright-brothers-were-most-definitely-the-first-in-flight-3903093, Accessed September 12, 2019.

Dayton Aviation Heritage National Park, https://www.nps.gov/daav/index.htm, Accessed September 12, 2019.

Huegel, Casey, "The Wright Brothers' Early Photography: A Research Note," *Ohio History*, 123, no. 1 (Spring 2016), pp. 73-87.

John T. Daniels, interview with *Collier's Weekly*, September 17, 1927, Smithsonian Education, http://www.smithsonianeducation.org/educators/lesson_plans/wright/group_d.html, Accessed August 30, 2019.

Mingos, Howard, "Up in the Air: When the Wright Brothers Learned to Fly," *Saturday Evening Post*, December 10, 2015, https://www.saturdayeveningpost.com/2015/12/air/, Accessed August 28, 2019.

Park, Edward, "Langley's "Feat—and Folly," Smithsonian.com, November 1997, https://www.smithsonianmag.com/history/langleys-feat-and-folly-145999254/, Accessed July 25, 2019.

Photography and the Wright Brothers. Wilbur and Orville Wright Papers at the Library of Congress, https://www.loc.gov/collections/wilbur-and-orville-wright-papers/articles-and-essays/photography-and-the-wright-brothers/, Accessed August 2, 2019.

Renstrom, Arthur George, *Wilbur & Orville Wright: A Reissue of a Chronology Commemorating the Hundredth Anniversary of the Birth of Orville Wright, August 19, 1871*, The U.S. Centennial of Flight Commission and the National Aeronautics and Space Administration, Monographs in Aerospace History, Number 32, September 2003, https://history.nasa.gov/monograph32.pdf, Accessed September 1, 2019.

The Sculpture, First Flight Foundation, https://firstflightfoundation.org/the-sculpture/, Accessed September 3, 2019.

Wright, Wilbur, and Orville Wright, "The Wright Brothers Aeroplane," *Century Magazine*, 76, no. 5 (September 1908), pp. 641-650.

Index

About the Author

Michael Burgan is a freelance writer who specializes in books for children and young adults, both fiction and nonfiction. A graduate of the University of Connecticut with a degree in history, Burgan is also a playwright and the editor of *The Biographer's Craft*, the newsletter for Biographers International Organization. He lives in Santa Fe, New Mexico.